Horn Solos
Book Two

Zweites Spielbuch für
Horn und Klavier

edited and arranged for horn and piano by
herausgegeben und bearbeitet für Horn und Klavier von

ARTHUR CAMPBELL

FABER MUSIC

Contents · Inhalt

Preface

Horn Solos Book Two continues the progressive series of pieces in Book One, to the point where the student can begin to tackle the standard sonata and concerto repertoire.

The book is designed to cover many of the technical problems encountered by the intermediate player, and the last two pieces have been included to introduce respectively hand-stopping and the bass clef.

As in Book One, many of the pieces are originally associated with the horn – background information and some ideas for interpretation will be found in the notes at the end of the horn part.

ARTHUR CAMPBELL

Vorwort

Das *Zweite Spielbuch für Hornsolos* führt die fortlaufende Serie der Stücke von Band 1 dahingehend weiter, daß der Spieler beginnen kann, Standartsonaten und Konzertrepertoires in Angriff zu nehmen.

Das Buch ist daraufhin konzipiert, daß viele der technischen Probleme, die dem Studenten der mittleren Stufe begegnen, in Angriff genommen werden. Die beiden letzten Stücke sind einbezogen, um sowohl die Technik des Handstopfens als auch den Baßschlüssel einzuführen.

Wie schon im ersten Buch, so sind auch diese Stücke ursprünglich für das Horn geschrieben – Hintergrundinformation und einige Hinweise zur Interpretation finden sich in den Anmerkungen am Ende des Hornteils.

ARTHUR CAMPBELL

1. EVENING PRAYER *(Hänsel und Gretel)*

Abendgebet

Engelbert Humperdinck
(1854–1921)
arr. Paul Reade

Calm, not too slow ♩ = 76

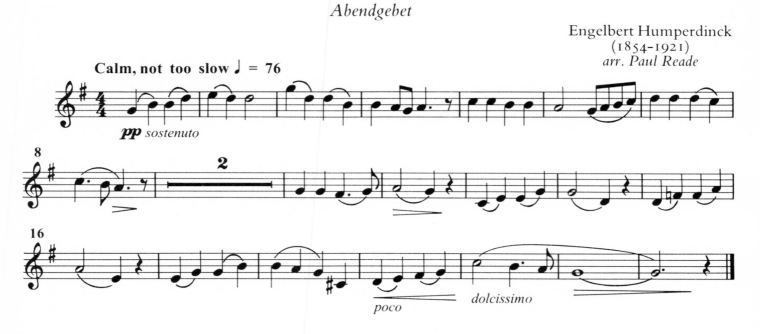

2. BROTHER, COME DANCE WITH ME
(Hänsel und Gretel)

Brüderchen, komm tanz mit mir

Engelbert Humperdinck
(1854–1921)

Allegretto con moto ♩ = 96

3. TO A WILD ROSE

An eine wilde Rose

Edward MacDowell
(1861–1908)
arr. Paul Reade

6

4. Ô MERVEILLE *(Faust)*

Charles François Gounod
(1818–1893)

5. SICILIENNE *(Pelléas et Mélisande)*

Gabriel Fauré
(1845–1924)

6. INAFFIA L'UGOLA! *(Otello)*

Giuseppe Verdi
(1813–1901)

8

7. SERENADE *(Don Procopio)*

Georges Bizet
(1838–1875)

Andantino quasi allegretto ♩. = 72

8. MEMORY *(Cats)*

Erinnerung

Andrew Lloyd Webber
(b. 1948)

Freely ♩. = 56

9. RECONDITA ARMONIA *(Tosca)*

Giacomo Puccini
(1858–1924)

10. HUNTING SONG *(Peasant Cantata)*
Jagdlied (Bauernkantate)

Johann Sebastian Bach
(1685–1750)

II. EN BATEAU

Claude Debussy
(1862–1918)

12. MIRTH ADMIT ME OF THY CREW (L'Allegro)

Laß mich, Freude, teilnehmen

George Frideric Handel
(1685–1759)

12

13. ECHO FANFARE
Echofanfare

Arthur Campbell

14. THEME FROM SYMPHONY NO. 2
Thema aus der Symphonie Nr. 2

Modern notation

Edward Elgar
(1857–1934)

Classical notation

NOTES

1. Humperdinck's opera *Hänsel und Gretel* is packed with horn music. *Evening Prayer*, sung by Hänsel and Gretel in the forest before they go to sleep, is also used as the introduction to the overture, where it is played by a quartet of horns.

2. Having been left at home to work, Gretel relieves their boredom by trying to teach Hänsel to dance, to the accompaniment of this charming tune.

3. The first of *Woodland Sketches*, a set of piano pieces by the American composer Edward MacDowell. It is a 'song without words' and it should be played in a simple style. The sharp key involves considerable use of the third finger; be sure to move the valve cleanly.

4. This horn solo from *Faust* accompanies a vision of Marguerite at her spinning wheel. Faust is so overcome by her beauty that he signs away his soul in exchange for renewed youth. Try to make your tone equally enchanting!

5. Fauré originally wrote this piece for cello and piano, then arranged it for orchestra as part of his incidental music to Maeterlinck's play, *Pelléas et Mélisande*. It needs smooth, gentle treatment with care for the phrasing.

6. A drinking song from *Otello*. Iago means to ruin Cassio by getting him drunk. The big tune at bar 24 is played by horns in the original score. The whole piece needs vigorous, even coarse, playing with the downward chromatic scales suggesting the reeling of a drunkard.

7. As a young man Bizet won the *Prix de Rome* and it was during his stay in the Italian capital that he wrote his opera *Don Procopio*. This serenade from the opera is accompanied by mandolin and guitar.

8. *Memory* is the most popular song from Andrew Lloyd Webber's musical, *Cats*. It suits the horn well. Be careful to play the quavers in the 4/8 bars at the same speed as those in 6/8.

9. An aria from Act 1 of *Tosca*, sung by the artist, Cavaradossi. He is addressing his portrait of Mary Magdalen in which he has incorporated the features of his lover, Tosca. This piece needs the passion of an Italian tenor and should be given plenty of *rubato*.

10. This piece, from Bach's *Peasant Cantata*, is based on a popular hunting song of the day and appears to have been included to honour a local nobleman who was keen on the chase.

11. *En bateau* comes from Debussy's *Petite Suite* for piano duet, although it is now better known in an orchestral arrangement. At the beginning and end the boat is drifting serenely downstream, but meets some more agitated water at bar 28. Be careful to play the rhythm of the duplets accurately.

12. Handel set a selection of verses from Milton's contrasting poems *l'Allegro* (cheerful) and *Il Penseroso* (melancholy). This one, from the former, is an aria for bass voice with horn obbligato and is about hunting. The original is a third higher.

13. A little study introducing you to the technique of hand-stopping. The main problem is intonation which depends on getting the correct open and closed hand positions. In this piece every stopped passage is first played 'open' for comparison.

14. This piece introduces the bass clef, which in horn music is used in two different ways. The more modern system uses the same transposition as for the treble clef (i.e. the music sounds a fifth lower than written), but classical composers always wrote bass clef notes an octave lower so that the music sounds a fourth higher than written. Sometimes it is necessary to refer to the full score to discover which convention is being used. Here, the horn part offers both versions for reading practice.

ANMERKUNGEN

1. Humperdincks Oper *Hänsel und Gretel* ist vollgepackt mit Hornmusik. Das *Abendgebet*, das von Hänsel und Gretel im Wald gesungen wird, ehe sie schlafen gehen, wird auch als Einführung zur Ouvertüre benutzt, in der es von einem Hornquartett gespielt wird.

2. Gretel, die zu Hause gelassen wurde, um zu arbeiten, versucht aus Langeweile Hänsel das Tanzen beizubringen zur Begleitung dieser zauberhaften Weise.

3. Bei der ersten der *Woodland Sketches* (*Waldszenen*) handelt es sich um einen Satz von Klavierstücken des amerikanischen Komponisten Edward MacDowell. Es ist ein einzelnes Lied ohne Worte und sollte in einfachem Stil gespielt werden. Die Dur-Tonart bringt den intensiven Gebrauch des dritten Fingers mit sich; achte auf saubere Klappenbedienung.

4. Dieses Hornsolo aus Faust begleitet eine Vision der Marguerite am Spinnrade. Faust ist so hingerissen von ihrer Schönheit, daß er seine Seele im Austausch für wiedergewonnene Jugend überschreibt. Versuche, den Ton ähnlich bezaubernd zu gestalten!

5. Fauré schrieb dieses Stück ursprünglich für Cello und Klavier und bearbeitete es dann für Orchester als Teil seiner Schauspielmusik für Maeterlincks Stück *Pelléas et Mélisande*. Es bedarf einer weichen, sanften Handhabung mit Vorsicht bei der Phrasierung.

6. Ein Trinklied aus *Otello*. Iago hat vor, Cassio zu vernichten, indem er ihn dazu bringt, sich zu betrinken. Die große Melodie in 24. Takt wird in der Originalfassung von Hörnern gespielt. Das ganze Stück bedarf des kräftigen, sogar groben Spiels, wobei die nach unten verlaufenden chromatischen Tonfolgen das Torkeln eines Betrunkenen andeuten.

7. Als junger Mann gewann Bizet den *Prix de Rome*, und dort schrieb er, während seines Aufenthaltes in der italienischen Hauptstadt, seine Oper *Don Procopio*. Diese Serenade aus der Oper wird von Mandoline und Gitarre begleitet.

8. *Memory* (*Erinnerung*) ist das populärste Lied aus Andrew Lloyd Webbers Musical *Cats* (*Katzen*). Es paßt gut zum Horn. Achte darauf, daß die Viertel in den 4/8 Takten mit gleichem Tempo wie die in den 6/8 Takten gespielt werden.

9. Eine Arie aus dem ersten Akt von *Tosca*, von dem Künstler Cavaradossi gesungen. Er richtet sie an sein Portrait der Maria Magdalena, in dem er die Züge seiner Geliebten Tosca festgehalten hat. Dieses Lied bedarf der Leidenschaft eines italienischen Tenors und sollte mit viel *rubato* gespielt werden.

10. Dieses Stück aus Bachs *Bauernkantate* basiert auf einem beliebten Jagdlied der damaligen Zeit und wurde wahrscheinlich zur Ehrung eines ansässigen Adeligen, der die Jagd liebte, mit einbegriffen.

11. *En Bâteau* stammt aus Debussys *Petite Suite* für Klavierduett, wenn es auch heute in der Orchesterbearbeitung besser bekannt ist. Am Anfang und am Ende treibt das Schiff ruhig den Fluß hinunter, aber im 28. Takt trifft es auf unruhigere Wasser. Achte darauf, den Rhythmus des Zweiertaktes akkurat zu spielen.

12. Händel schrieb die Musik zu einen Teil der Verse von Miltons vergleichenden Gedichten *L'Allegro* (freudig) und *Il Penseroso* (traurig). Dieses Stück, ein Teil des ersten Gedichts, ist eine Arie für Baß mit Obligatstimme des Horns und dreht sich um die Jagd. Die Originalversion ist ein drittel höher.

13. Eine kleine Studie, die die Technik des Handstopfens einführt. Das Hauptproblem bietet die Intonation, die von der korrekten 'offenen' und 'geschlossenen' Handposition abhängt. In diesem Stück ist jede gestopfte Passage zunächst zum besseren Vergleich 'offen' gespielt.

14. Dieses Stück führt den Baßschlüssel ein, der in der Hornmusik auf zwei verschiedene Weisen benutzt wird. Das modernere System benutzt die gleiche Transposition wie für den Diskantschlüssel (d.h. die Musik klingt um ein fünftel tiefer als in der Notierung). Klassische Komponisten schrieben den Baßschlüssel jedoch eine Oktave tiefer, so daß die Musik ein viertel höher klang als die Notierung. Es ist manchmal notwendig die Gesamtpartitur heranzuziehen, um herauszufinden, welcher Konvention gefolgt wurde. Hier bietet der Hornteil beide Versionen.

Horn Solos
Book Two

*Zweites Spielbuch für
Horn und Klavier*

edited and arranged for horn and piano by
herausgegeben und bearbeitet für Horn und Klavier von

ARTHUR CAMPBELL

© 1992 by Faber Music Limited
First published in 1992 by Faber Music Ltd
3 Queen Square London WC1N 3AU
Cover design by Roslav Szaybo and Studio Gerrard
Printed in England

FABER MUSIC

Contents · Inhalt

Preface

Horn Solos Book Two continues the progressive series of pieces in Book One, to the point where the student can begin to tackle the standard sonata and concerto repertoire.

The book is designed to cover many of the technical problems encountered by the intermediate player, and the last two pieces have been included to introduce respectively hand-stopping and the bass clef.

As in Book One, many of the pieces are originally associated with the horn – background information and some ideas for interpretation will be found in the notes at the end of the horn part.

ARTHUR CAMPBELL

Vorwort

Das *Zweite Spielbuch für Hornsolos* führt die fortlaufende Serie der Stücke von Band 1 dahingehend weiter, daß der Spieler beginnen kann, Standartsonaten und Konzertrepertoires in Angriff zu nehmen.

Das Buch ist daraufhin konzipiert, daß viele der technischen Probleme, die dem Studenten der mittleren Stufe begegnen, in Angriff genommen werden. Die beiden letzten Stücke sind einbezogen, um sowohl die Technik des Handstopfens als auch den Baßschlüssel einzuführen.

Wie schon im ersten Buch, so sind auch diese Stücke ursprünglich für das Horn geschrieben – Hintergrundinformation und einige Hinweise zur Interpretation finden sich in den Anmerkungen am Ende des Hornteils.

ARTHUR CAMPBELL

1. EVENING PRAYER *(Hänsel und Gretel)*

Abendgebet

Engelbert Humperdinck
(1854–1921)
arr. *Paul Reade*

2. BROTHER, COME DANCE WITH ME
(Hänsel und Gretel)

Brüderchen, komm tanz mit mir

Engelbert Humperdinck
(1854–1921)

3. TO A WILD ROSE

An eine wilde Rose

Edward MacDowell
(1861–1908)
arr. Paul Reade

4. Ô MERVEILLE *(Faust)*

Charles François Gounod
(1818–1893)

9

5. SICILIENNE *(Pelléas et Mélisande)*

Gabriel Fauré
(1845–1924)

6. INAFFIA L'UGOLA! *(Otello)*

Giuseppe Verdi
(1813–1901)

7. SERENADE *(Don Procopio)*

Georges Bizet
(1838–1875)

8. MEMORY (Cats)

Erinnerung

Andrew Lloyd Webber
(b. 1948)

9. RECONDITA ARMONIA *(Tosca)*

Giacomo Puccini
(1858–1924)

10. HUNTING SONG *(Peasant Cantata)*

Jagdlied (Bauernkantate)

Johann Sebastian Bach
(1685–1750)

II. EN BATEAU

Claude Debussy
(1862–1918)

12. MIRTH ADMIT ME OF THY CREW *(L'Allegro)*

Laß mich, Freude, teilnehmen

George Frideric Handel
(1685–1759)

13. ECHO FANFARE

Echofanfare

Arthur Campbell

14. THEME FROM SYMPHONY NO. 2
Thema aus der Symphonie Nr. 2

Edward Elgar
(1857–1934)

* *The horn cue line uses modern bass clef notation.*
The separate horn part also includes classical bass clef notation.